SHADOWTIME

SHADOWTIME

Libretto by
charles bernstein

Music by
brian ferneyhough

GREEN INTEGER
KØBENHAVN & LOS ANGELES
2005

GREEN INTEGER BOOKS
Edited by Per Bregne
København / Los Angeles

Distributed in the United States by Consortium Book
Sales and Distribution, 1045 Westgate Drive, Suite 90
Saint Paul, Minnesota 55114-1065
Distributed in England and throughout Europe by
Turnaround Publisher Services
Unit 3, Olympia Trading Estate
Coburg Road, Wood Green, London N22 6TZ
44 (0)20 88293009

(323) 857-1115 / http://www.greeninteger.com

First Green Integer Edition 2005
Libretto copyright ©2005, 2004 by Charles Bernstein
Design: Per Bregne
Typography: Kim Silva
Cover photograph of Charles Bernstein
Back cover copy copyright ©2005 by Green Integer

LIBRARY OF CONGRESS CATALOGING IN PUBLICATION DATA
Bernstein, Charles [1950]
Shadowtime
ISBN: 1-933382-00-7
p. cm – Green Integer 122
I. Title II. Series

Green Integer books are published for Douglas Messerli
Printed in the United States on acid-free paper

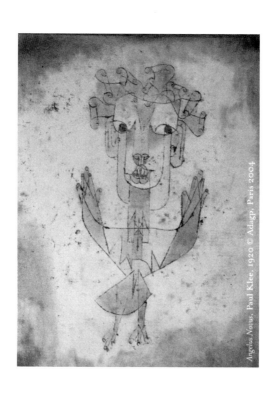

Paul Klee, *Angelus Novus*

TABLE OF CONTENTS

ACKNOWLEDGEMENTS

Shadowtime was commissioned by the City of Munich for the Münchener Biennale and premiered in Munich on May 25, 2004, at Prinzregententheater. In October 2004, the production traveled to Festival d'Automne à Paris, Théâtre Nanterre-Amandiersin. *Shadowtime* will be performed at the Lincoln Center Festival in New York in July 2005. The musical director for these performances is Jurjen Hempel and the stage director is Frédéric Fisbach.

I wrote much of the synopsis after the Munich performances. It reflects my response to first seeing the production and to first hearing the score performed. (For images from, and reviews of, the production, visit the *Shadowtime* website at epc.buffalo.edu/authors/bernstein/shadowtime.)

The complete musical score for the opera is published by Peters Editions. Thanks especially to Fiona Flower and Marc Dooley at Peters for their assistance. Graham Hayter helped me with all the formal arrangements for the opera through his agency Contemporary Music Promotions. His generosity, and support for new music, is much appreciated.

In the Spring of 1999, on a visit I made to the University of California, San Diego, Brian Ferney-hough asked if I would like to write a libretto for an opera he had been commissioned to write. Brian explained that he wanted the opera to center on the work of Walter Benjamin. I immediately agreed and over the next few months we set to work collaborating on the overall structure for the work. I wrote much of the libretto in 1999, while Brian continued to compose the score until short-ly before the Munich premiere, five years later. Brian also wrote several key passages in the libret-to: the two initial texts in Scene I and the opening text of Scene IV. To say that the libretto is written both for, and in collaboration with, Brian Ferney-hough only begins to touch on my debt to him and my appreciation for his music, which inspired this work at every level and in every detail.

I was fortunate to work with two translators – Juliette Valéry for the French and Benedikt Lede-bur for the German – who contributed greatly to this project, creating parallel works of their own, and also contributing to some significant emendations of the libretto. Even in this English version of the text, the mark of the translators is present.

Sections of the libretto have been published by *boundary 2, The Boston Review, The Notre Dame Review, West Coast Line, Performance Research,* and *The Forward.*

Douglas Messerli, from my first books to this one, my first book with Green Integer, has been a ready companion and a steady friend.

Finally, Joséphine Markovits, our angel, brought the opera from the heavens to earth; her support, through the Festival d'Automne, has been foundational to the project.

C.B.

GUILFORD, CONN., AUGUST 16, 2004

SYNOPSIS

Shadowtime is a "thought opera" based on the work and life of Walter Benjamin (1892-1940). Benjamin is one of the greatest philosophers and cultural critics of the twentieth century. Born in Berlin, he died on the Spanish border while trying to escape the fate that awaited most of his fellow Central European Jews. In its seven scenes, *Shadowtime* explores some of the major themes of Benjamin's work, including the intertwined natures of history, time, transience, timelessness, language, and melancholy; the possibilities for a transformational leftist politics; the interconnectivity of language, things, and cosmos; and the role of dialectical materiality, aura, interpretation, and translation in art. Beginning on the last evening of Benjamin's life, *Shadowtime* projects an alternative course for what happened on that fateful night. Opening onto a world of shades, of ghosts, of the dead, *Shadowtime* inhabits a period in human history in which the light flickered and then failed.

Scenes

I. New Angels/Transient Failures (Prologue)
  Level 1: Lecturer
  Level 2: Radio (1940)
  Level 3: War Time (Spanish Border, 1940):
    Innkeeper, Henny Gurland, Benjamin, Doctor
  Level 4: Reflective Time (Memory + Thought)
    (Berlin, 1917): Benjamin in dialog with Dora
    Kellner (Benjamin)
  Level 5: Five Rimes for Stefan Benjamin
  Level 6: Redemptive Time (Triple Lecture):
    Benjamin in separate dialogs with Gershom
    Scholem and Hölderlin (who appears as a
    pseudo-Benjamin and as Scardanelli)

II. Les Froissements d'Ailes de Gabriel
  (First Barrier) (instrumental)

III. The Doctrine of Similarity (13 Canons)
    1. Amphibolies I (Walk Slowly)
    2. Dust to Dusk
    3. Cannot Cross
    4. Indissolubility (Motetus absconditus)
    5. Amphibolies II (Noon)

Summary

SCENE I – In September 1940, one step ahead of the Nazi invaders, Walter Benjamin fled France, taking an arduous journey, on foot, over the Pyrenees mountains. He died the day after his arrival in Spain. Benjamin's final day is the central motif of the prologue, "New Angels/Transient Failures." "New Angels" refers to the Paul Klee painting, "Angelus Novus," which Benjamin writes about in "On the Concept of History." The scene opens with some metaphysical speculations by a quixotic Lecturer, a mercurial figure who reappears in Scenes IV and VI. Scene I has several overlapping layers and is presided over by the chorus, whose members represent the Angels of History.

The primary layer, "War Time," takes center stage. The setting is just over the French border, in the Pyrenees, at the hotel, Fonda de Francia, Portbou, Spain. The time is just before midnight, September 25, 1940. Benjamin has arrived at the hotel with his traveling companion Henny Gurland. The trip had been made more difficult by

Benjamin's bad heart: every ten minutes of walking was followed by one minute of stopping. Benjamin's plan was to continue on to Lisbon, and from there to America. But the Innkeeper informs Benjamin and Gurland that their transit visas have been voided and that they must return to France (and to the dark destiny that would await them). At center stage, the cruel Innkeeper gives the exhausted travelers the bad news, to Gurland's protests and Benjamin's growing despair. The Lecturer, now in the guise of a doctor, enters the scene. Having been called to the hotel because of the alarming state of Benjamin's health, the doctor says Benjamin must rest.

Meanwhile, on the right side of the stage, at the same time as the central scene from Benjamin's last hours, a dialog takes place, in flashback, between the young Benjamin and his wife, Dora Kellner. This layer, called "Reflective Time (Memory + Thought)," is set in Berlin around 1917, the year of their marriage. The dialog focuses on their shared aspirations, in their youth, for the radical German student movement of the years immediately prior to World War I, and touches on the nature of emotion, eros, and prostitution.

Another layer consists of five short children's "rimes" (dedicated to Benjamin's son Stefan, who was born in 1918), performed by a quartet from the chorus.

The final layer is a triple lecture called "Redemptive Time." It follows the dialog with Dora and occurs simultaneously with the central 1940 scene. This layer has two parts: a philosophical, political, and theological dialog with Benjamin's closest friend Gershom Scholem, the great historian of Jewish mysticism; and a dialog with Friedrich Hölderlin, the German poet of the late eighteenth and early nineteenth century, who was important to Benjamin. The text of these two dialogs are unfurled on stage from large scrolls.

SCENE 11 – "Les Froissements d'Ailes de Gabriel" (The Rustling of the Wings of Gabriel) is instrumental, scored for solo guitar and thirteen players. The guitar suggests the just audible, transitory, flickering, chimerical rustling of the wings of Gabriel, the angel of Messianic time. This is *Shadowtime's* first barrier, marking the beginning of the journey of Benjamin's avatar (shadow or dream figure) from the represented historical times of Scene I to the nonhistorical time of the unfolding opera.

SCENE III – "The Doctrine of Similarity" – consists of thirteen short movements, sung by various groupings of the chorus of the Angels of History. Each of the movements reflects on the nature of history, time, and translation/transformation. The title comes from an essay by Benjamin with a similar name –"Doctrine of the Similar"– in which he considers the ways that the physical sounds of language echo or mimic the primordial structures of the cosmos. In the scene, various numeric patterns create reverberations within and between the text and music. The theme of temporality is explored musically by the use of canon forms throughout the scene. Canons 1, 5 and 12 are called "Amphibolies," suggesting mineral ambiguities, where "pricks are points on a map" and "where shadows are thickest at noon." Canons 2 and 11 have the same text, which ripples from one end of the chorus to the other: "The leaves turn dark before the trees are shot with light." Canon 3 is a lyric both lamentory and defiant. In canon 4, "Indissolubility," the concern with the temporal is represented by the choice of a multiple, palimpsestic parody of a late medieval motet from the Montpelier Codex. The libretto extends these investigations through the use of linguistic translations and displacements. While the text roams in time, space, and content, it returns to the knotted dead-end situations of life in extremity, as in canon 6, "In the Dark," and canon 7: "Sometimes / you burn a book because / It is cold / and you need the fire / to keep warm / and / sometimes / you read a / book for the same reason." Canon 8, "Anagrammatica," consists entirely of anagrams of Benjamin's name. Canon 9, "dew and die" is a homophonic (sound) translation of a poem by Ernst Jandl, while canon 10 refers to a key Benjamin concept: *schein*. The last canon, 13, is based on the final stanza of Mallarmé's "Salute."

SCENE IV – "Opus Contra Naturam (Descent of Benjamin into the Underworld)," a shadow play for speaking pianist, is the pivotal scene of *Shad-*

owtime, inaugurating the second half of the opera. "Opus Contra Naturam" is an alchemical term for work against, or beyond, the constraints of nature. The Lecturer from Scene I appears in guise of a Joker or Liberace-like singer in a Las Vegas piano bar (that suggests also a Weimar cabaret). He leads Benjamin's avatar, set adrift after the fateful events of September 1940, on the Orphic descent into a shadow world ("katabasis") of shock-induced paralysis ("kataplexy").

SCENE V – In the darkly surreal "Pools of Darkness (11 Interrogations)," Benjamin's avatar is interrogated by a series of haunting, masked figures. Each interrogation is set to a distinct musical form. Three Giant Mouths (Canon/Heterophony) question the Benjamin figure about the nature of the future; a Headless Ghoul (Isorhythmic Motet) asks about dreaming; the two-headed figure of Karl Marx and Groucho Marx joined to the body of Kerberus (Hoquetus/Melodrama) taunts Benjamin's avatar about the nature of memory; Benjamin's contemporary Pope Pius XII (Dramatic Madrigal a Due) wonders if his fate is part of

God's plan; Joan of Arc (Palimpsestic Chorale) worries about the fate of history; the Baal Shem Tov, disguised as a vampire (Rebus), poses a series of impossible comparisons, such as "Is assimilation better than estrangement?"; Adolf Hitler (Rondo) considers the nature of existence; Albert Einstein (Passacaglia cum Figuris in Eco) asks "What time is it *now*?," a Border Guard (Pastoral Interlude) makes the standard interrogation; Four Furies (Fugato) ask "What is to be done?" and receive the reply: "The light spills into pools of darkness. I can no longer find it." Finally, the Golem (Quodlibet/Abgesangszena) asks a set of menacing questions in an invented language; the final response is from a line of Heine: "Keine Kaddish wird man sagen" ("no one to say Kaddish for me").

SCENE VI – In the second and final barrier of *Shadowtime,* the Lecturer reappears, in a new guise, to perform "Seven Tableaux Vivants Representing the Angel of History as Melancholia." Both Scene VI and VII imagine Benjamin's Angel of History as the angel depicted in Albrecht Dürer's 1514 engraving, "Melencolia," which shows a dejected, winged figure, surrounded by instruments of scientific inquiry. Tableaux 1 and 4 are reworkings of two poems by the nineteenth-century, German-Jewish, post-Romantic poet Heinrich Heine, a distant relative of Benjamin's. Both poems are standards of the lieder repertoire, previously set by many composers – "Der Tod, das ist die Kühle Nacht" and "Die Lorelei." (Heine's work was censored and banned by the Nazis.) Tableau 2, "Tensions," is a series of sound translations of ten-word propositions, as, for example, "each ear's sly fiction a toy taboo which founds us." Tableau 3 is based on permutations of phrases from Benjamin's essay "Hashish in Marseilles": "Seeing only nuances." Tableau 5, "One and a Half Truths," takes its title from one of Benjamin's favorite contemporaries, aphorist Karl Kraus; it is a set of imaginary epigrams, concluding "Truth / Is a gun loaded with a parachute." Tableau 6 presents a full set of syntactic rotations of the sentence, "if you can't see it it can still hurt you." The final tableau ends with a play on negative dialectics, asking "whether what is is so because / Is so because it's not."

SCENE VII – "Stelae for Failed Time," the epilogue, is an elegiac solo by the Angel of History (imagined as the angel in Dürer's "Melencolia"). The angelic chorus sings to and for Benjamin. For the Angel of History, the song has a single voice; in the historical time of the performance, this solo is splintered into the many voices –the angels – of the chorus. "Stelae for Failed Time" has two overlapping layers. The first is a reflection on time and uncertainty in the context of historical recrimination and erasure: "I back away / helpless, my / eyes fixed. / This is my task: / to imagine no wholes / from all that has been smashed." In a lyric that echoes a lover's lament for her lost lover, the first layer ends with an evocation of one of Benjamin's central concerns, the radical break with historical time into "now time" *(Jetztzeit)*. The second layer is a reflection on representation: "The best picture / of a picture / is not a picture / but the negative" and ends on the theme of failed – and falling – time: "as now you fall / from my arms / into my capacious / insomniac forgetting."

I. NEW ANGELS / TRANSIENT FAILURES (PROLOGUE)

Setting: On the French border at the hotel, Fonda
de Francia, Portbou, Spain
Just before midnight, September 25, 1940

Level 1: Lecturer

According to Aristotle the word "blind" cannot be applied to men, moles and stones in exactly the same sense. Scheler argues that the pragmatic certainty of our own death arises from the observation that advancing age constricts the possibilities available to us often converging at the limit of a single possibility or of none at all. Understanding of Being reveals itself as the innermost ground of our finitude. Ontology is an index of finitude. Once grasped the finitude of existence brings Dasein into the simplicity of its fate.

Level 2: Radio (1940)

[Single voices from chorus:]

Geisteswissenschaften. Nur hinseh'n. Verbergung. Unheimliche Langeweile.
Aletheia. Die drei Schleier bei sich.
Destruktionsproblematikgleichursprünglichinswerksetzenwerbinich?
Schuldig sein.
Der letzte Gott - Eine Weise des Setzens, die ontologische Differenz.
Umriss. Die Zerklüftung. Der Verweser. Ruinanz.
Geschick / Genick. Umriss / Aufriss / Grundriss zumeist?
Anamnesis (Aussagelogik unwesentlich).

Dream rehearsing third-age regime
Midget threading, greet herding! Aim! Engird hermit!
Nightair thing emerged, art hinged Genieregime in age, righter.
Grim heritage-erg, nightmare harm ingather.

Die drei Schleier sind:
  Die Berechnung,
  Die Geschwindigkeit und
  Die Seinsverlassenheit.

Grund / Abgrund

Nihil sine ratione
Zuhause.
Der Horizont enden lassen.
Umkippung.

Extase der Nichtung / Sein zum Tode /
  Das Menschenmaterial.

Philosophische Auseinandersetzung als
  Destruktion oder:
Die Beständigkeit, die Grundstimmung eines
  Gestells.

Intuitus originarius / Intuitus variatus

Hate-heart mange: dig here, German
  emigrant!

Das Wofür-derangement-Spielraum, Das
  Geschick – Gegenstand der Entbergung.
Ruhe. Augenblickstätte. Ganzseinkönnen. Die
  Züchtigung vom zureichenden Grund.

[All chorus members:]

Und nun: die Vorstellung!

Angry hydra held her hand redly
Ran hung red lung
Held nary dry hand
Henna redly her gun land

Level 3: War Time (Spanish Border, 1940)

Innkeeper
Henny Gurland
Doctor
Walter Benjamin

INNKEEPER:
I regret to inform you

Herr Benjamin, Frau Gurland
but I must inform you
Frau Gurland, Herr Benjamin
you will understand
Herr Benjamin, Frau Gurland
it is my duty to inform you
Frau Gurland, Herr Benjamin
that your transit visas
Herr Benjamin, Frau Gurland
your transit visas
Frau Gurland, Herr Benjamin
are not valid
Herr Benjamin, Frau Gurland
you may not travel in Spain.
Frau Gurland, Herr Benjamin
You and your party
Herr Benjamin, Frau Gurland
must to return to France
Frau Gurland, Herr Benjamin
you will return to France
Herr Benjamin, Frau Gurland
in the morning.

HENNY GURLAND:
Our plan is to go on
to go on
to Lisbon
to Lisbon by train
and from there by plane
by plane from Lisbon
to America.
We shall go on
to America.
We do not wish to
stay in Spain
this is for us
a place of transit
from which
we shall go on
a place of transit
from which
we shall go on
go on
to America.

WALTER BENJAMIN:
Time is running out.

The last grains
fall from the hourglass
by ones and one
one and ones.
The grains fall
from the hourglass
all the time in the world
one by one
ticking off the seconds
one by one by one by one.

HENNY GURLAND:
Our papers are in order.
Please check again.
Our papers are in order.
We were told
these transit visas
guaranteed safe passage.
This is what we were told.
This is what we understood.
Safe passage through Spain
is all we want.
We have walked so long
through the mountains

all day
through the mountains.
All we ask is
what we were told.
Safe passage only.
We are on our way
to America.
The Americans
have said
we may go there.
Our papers are in order.
Please check again.
All we ask is
what we were told.
To America
we are on our way
to America.

WB:
Listen to the count run out
1, 2, 3, 4, 5, 6, 7, 8, 9, 10
now take a stop and once more
1, 3, 2, 4, 8, 5, 10, 6, 7, 9
another stop, again,
9, 6, 4, 5, 8, 3, 2, 7, 1, 10.

INNKEEPER:
We are a nation of laws
Herr Benjamin, Frau Gurland
and a nation of laws
Frau Gurland, Herr Benjamin
makes no exceptions.
Herr Benjamin, Frau Gurland
No exceptions.
Frau Gurland, Herr Benjamin
Exceptions
Herr Benjamin, Frau Gurland
trample on
Frau Gurland, Herr Benjamin
they trample on
Herr Benjamin, Frau Gurland
what we hold
Frau Gurland, Herr Benjamin
we hold
Herr Benjamin, Frau Gurland
most sacred.
Frau Gurland, Herr Benjamin
I do my duty
Herr Benjamin, Frau Gurland
by following the orders

Frau Gurland, Herr Benjamin
of my conscience
Herr Benjamin, Frau Gurland
and of the state.
Frau Gurland, Herr Benjamin
For this
Herr Benjamin, Frau Gurland
is what I hold
Frau Gurland, Herr Benjamin
most high
Herr Benjamin, Frau Gurland
most sacred.
Frau Gurland, Herr Benjamin
I do not expect you
Herr Benjamin, Frau Gurland
who have no state
Frau Gurland, Herr Benjamin
no land that is yours
Herr Benjamin, Frau Gurland
to understand
Frau Gurland, Herr Benjamin
that this is my duty
Herr Benjamin, Frau Gurland
my sacred duty

Frau Gurland, Herr Benjamin
to God and my country
Herr Benjamin, Frau Gurland.

WB:
No way out. No
way to go on.
Place your bets
place your bets now.
Put your chips
on the cracks
between
the numbers
and the ball
will be sure
to fall
on either side.
Place your bets
place your bets now
red or black
place your bets
in the cracks.
Last chance.
No way out

nor way to
go on.
Watch now
the ball rolls
round and round
round and round.
No way out.
The winner's
the one lives
to tell the tale.

HENNY GURLAND:
But please, can't you
can't you
can't you please
contact the American consulate.
Have you
no decency?
The American consulate will help.
Our papers are in order.
Please check again.
We have safe passage.
We were told
these transit visas

38

guaranteed safe passage.
This we were told.
This we understood.
No decency.
Have you, none,
no decency?

WB *(counting)*:
Each minute I count
every fourth number to 360
and then back again to zero
back again to now.
I count to lose track of the hour
but the hour never loses track.
Then back again to zero
back again to now.
I hear the ticking of the clock
the ticking of the clock
as if I were
on the other side of time
staring in.

INNKEEPER:
Herr Benjamin, Frau Gurland

I must inform you
Frau Gurland, Herr Benjamin
you will understand
Herr Benjamin, Frau Gurland
it is my duty to inform you
Frau Gurland, Herr Benjamin
we have called the American consulate
Herr Benjamin, Frau Gurland
but they will not intervene.
Frau Gurland, Herr Benjamin
It is my duty to inform you
Herr Benjamin, Frau Gurland
even the Americans recognize
Frau Gurland, Herr Benjamin
the rule of law
Herr Benjamin, Frau Gurland
as the basis of civilization.

DOCTOR *(Listens for heart rate: sound of an
erratic beat):*
Señor Benjamin's
heart is weak
the beat irregular.

HENNY GURLAND:
During the journey …
the rhythm of his walk …
we would go for ten minutes
then stop for one …
all day long we proceeded
in this way, ten minutes forward,
one minute stopped …
we would go
in this way
one minute stopped
ten minutes forward
during the journey
all day long
the rhythm of his walk
we proceeded
then stop for one
in this way
the rhythm
ten minutes forward
during the journey
all day long
in this way
we proceeded

then stop for one
stop for one
in this way
the rhythm.

DOCTOR:
Señor Benjamin must rest tonight.
I will return tomorrow and check his condition
    again.
I have done all I can do for the moment.
Goodnight.

WB:
The future seems certain
certain
to go on
without us.
The future seems certain
to go on
go on
the future seems
to go on
without us
future certain

seems certain
to go
without us.

Level 4: Reflective Time (Memory + Thought)
   (Berlin, 1917)

   Dora Kellner (later Dora Benjamin)
   The Young Walter Benjamin

KELLNER:
The poverty of student life
makes for the riches
of an order of conformity
that endangers even the dead.

YOUNG WB:
Our task is to liberate the future
from its deformed existence
in the womb of the present.

KELLNER:
You can do nothing worthwhile
until you discover your own imperatives
the commands that will make
the supreme demands on your life.

YOUNG WB:
Only for the sake of the hopeless
have we been given hope.

KELLNER:
And are we the hopeless
or the ones given hope?

YOUNG WB:
It is not just women
who prostitute themselves.

KELLNER:
Either all people
are prostitutes
or no one is.

YOUNG WB:
We all are
for we are all
objects and subjects
of culture.

KELLNER:
And Eros …

YOUNG WB:
Eros is the god …

KELLNER:
most hostile to culture.

YOUNG WB:
Yet even Eros can be perverted.
Even Eros can serve culture.

KELLNER:
And emotion?
Tell me about emotion.
How it waxes and weaves
and wobbles and wanes,

how it's there
and then vanishes
or transforms itself
into what was never there
before?

YOUNG WB:
The more deeply
emotion
understands itself
the more
it is understood
as transition.
Emotion
is the
trace
of a
moment
in time.
It
never
signifies
an
end.

KELLNER:

I hold tight
but find
in my arms
only
the past.

YOUNG WB:

The tears which fill your eyes
deprive them of the physical world.
For what transpires now
has never before been
and is already gone
as you reflect on it.

KELLNER:

It is early morning …

YOUNG WB:

and the sea is roaring …

KELLNER:

outside the window.

Level 5: Five Rimes for Stefan Benjamin

Four Children

Jump over sticks
Jump over stones
But better be sure
Not to break your bones

Down in the dumps
Up in the mud
Tell your mother
To take you home

Silly you, silly we
Cat's got your tongue
Don't blame it on me

Inside out not outside in
Our neighbor's in the tool shed
Drinking blood like gin

Beat your wings
Against the stars

You'll still fall down
Whoever you are

Level 6: Redemptive Time (Triple Lecture)

Part One

Gershom Scholem
WB

wb:
It is characteristic
Of philosophical writing
That it must
Continually confront questions
Of representation

scholem:
There are 49
Layers of meaning
In every passage
Of the *Talmud*

WB:

Language as such, that is the text
That we interpret
And that interprets us

SCHOLEM:

Are you ready to be the new Rashi
Raising commentary to new heights
So that the art of criticism
Becomes a sacred process
Releasing the sparks inside the words?

WB:

Critique cannot confine itself to letters
But must also confront
That which animates the letters

SCHOLEM:

And how can we grasp
What animates the letters?

WB:

It is never enough to grasp
But also to grapple

SCHOLEM:

Do you mean to put divinity on trial?

WB:

I am the prosecutor
Who will put divinity on trial
For breach of contract.
For God promised a Messiah
But no Messiah comes

SCHOLEM:

Comes to whom?
Who can say
How the Messiah's presence
Emanates
Or how it is hidden?

WB:

I speak of the Messiah whom the poet
Senses without naming, the painter
Feels without seeing, the composer
Hears without noting, the philosopher
Supposes without knowing

SCHOLEM:

And in what court can the Heavenly be judged?

WB:

In the court of critique

SCHOLEM:

And who can judge the Nameless?

WB:

Only the living who live in its shadow

SCHOLEM:

And what if the living refuse to convict
That which they have yet to know

WB:

If we can't convict God
Then let's indict the bourgeoisie
For they promise a utopia
That never comes, exploiting
Each according to their ability
To be exploited, making commodities

Of all that could have been
Sparks of hope

SCHOLEM:
Metaphysics and materialism
Are the peas in your shell game
And you are the Adventurer King
Of Ambiguity and Obscurity
Skimming the textual profits
From the fragments you have gleaned

WB:
I know my vacillations
Janus-faced
Make strange connections
I go full throttle in one direction
Then arc my thought
Against itself, a bow forever
Waiting for an arrow

SCHOLEM:
Self-deception can lead only to suicide

WB:

Better a bad revolutionary
Than a good bourgeois

SCHOLEM:

Yet I perceive the method
Refusing to be bound
By all that cripples thought

WB:

A way to think
Outside the self-enclosing circles
That bury us alive and make us
Deaf even to the dead

SCHOLEM:

This is why we sing the lamentations

WB:

But how can language ever fulfill itself
As mourning?

SCHOLEM:
It is not the exterior expression
But the inner process

WB:
Then mourning is a kind of listening
Where the dead sing to us
And even the living tell their stories

•

Part Two

Benjamin (Hölderlin as a pseudo-Benjamin)
Hölderlin (as Scardanelli)

BENJAMIN:
In the context of poetic density
All figures acquire identity

HÖLDERLIN:
Near is
And difficult to grasp

BENJAMIN:
The impenetrability of relation resists
Every mode of comprehension
Other than that of feeling

HÖLDERLIN:
Your foot, does it not walk
On what is true, as upon carpets?

BENJAMIN:
The poeticized, which is identical with life –

HÖLDERLIN:
You are a lonely deer.
Your timidity is your way
Of entering the world.
This is your courage.

BENJAMIN:
And after? What awaits?

HÖLDERLIN:
Nothing waits
But the motionless space

Between things
To which you surrender
As song

BENJAMIN:
Death a veil
That opens
Onto a void

HÖLDERLIN:
In which the heavenly
Gathers itself

BENJAMIN:
Radiantly porous

HÖLDERLIN:
Sacredly sober

BENJAMIN:
But beauty
Is never in the lifting
Of a veil.

It is the secret
Of its enfolding.

HÖLDERLIN:
Are not the living –
Many of them –
Known to you?

BENJAMIN:
What is alive
Can be perceived
Only by means
Of what is not.
The dead speak
But only the living
Hear them.

HÖLDERLIN:
Returning, forming into itself, coming home –

Notes

The texts of Level 1, for the Lecturer, and Level II, for Radio, are by Brian Ferneyhough.

The children's rimes in the fifth layer are dedicated to Benjamin's son Stefan (born 1918).

In the set of dialogs in the sixth layer, Scardenelli is an alternate persona for Hölderlin; Hölderlin used this pseudonym for the poems he wrote in the Tübigen Tower.

Source for biographical information: *Walter Benjamin: A Biography* by Momme Brodersen, tr. Malcolm R. Green and Ingrida Ligers (London: Verso, 1996).

II. LES FROISSEMENTS D'AILES
DE GABRIEL (FIRST BARRIER)
(INSTRUMENTAL)

Notes

"Angelus Novus" ("New Angel") is the title of a 1910 Paul Klee painting purchased by Benjamin in 1921. That same year Benjamin planned to use the name as the title of a journal that never materialized. This image recurs, in Scenes VI and VII, as the "Angel of History." Benjamin discusses the painting in "On the Concept of History":

> My wing is poised to beat
> but I would gladly return home
> were I to stay to the end of days
> I would still be this forlorn
> – Gershom Scholem, "Greetings from Angelus"
> [tr. Richard Sieburth]

There is a painting by Klee called *Angelus Novus*. It shows an angel who seems about to move away from something he stares at. His eyes are wide, his mouth is open, his wings are spread. This is how the angel of history must look. His face is turned toward the past. Where a chain of events appears before *us, he* sees one single catastrophe, which keeps piling wreckage upon wreckage and hurls it at his feet. The angel would like to stay, awaken the dead, and make whole what has been smashed. But a storm is blowing from Paradise and has got caught in his wings; it is so strong that the angel can no longer close them. This storm drives him irresistibly into the future to which his back is turned, while the pile of debris before him grows toward the sky. What we call progress is *this* storm.

– from Walter Benjamin's 1940 work, "On the Concept of History," *Gesammelte Schriften* (Frankfurt am Main: Suhrkamp Verlag, 1974), 1: 691-704. Translation: Harry Zohn, from Walter Benjamin, *Selected Writings,* Vol. 4: 1938-1940 (Cambridge: Harvard University Press, 2003), 392-93. Scholem's poem on the Klee painting was written for Benjamin's twenty-ninth birthday – July 15, 1921. Sieburth's translation is from Gershom Scholem, *The Fullness of Time: Poems* (Jerusalem: Ibis Editions, 2003).

III. THE DOCTRINE OF SIMILARITY
(13 CANONS)

1. Amphibolies I (Walk Slowly)

Walk slowly
and jump quickly
over
the paths into
the
briar. The
pricks are points on a
map
that take
you back behind the stares
where shadows are
thickest at
noon.

•

Fault no lease
add thump whimsy
aver
a sash onto
a
mire. The
sticks are loins on a
gap
not fake
rude facts remind a fear
tear tallow mar
missed ease at
loom.

•

Balk sulky
ant hump prick fee
clover
an ash injure
at-
tire. The
flicks are joints on a
nap

(nutmeg)
glue's knack refines the dare
near fallow bars
quickest latch
gone.

2. Dust to Dusk

The leaves turn dark before the trees are shot
    with light.

3. Cannot Cross

When winds of change are gone
Blasts of fear take hold
Don't want consolation
Just a ticket home

It's been so long
Words cannot console us
Where there is sorrow
We cannot cross

A song is coming
Can find no rest
We cannot cross
Give us the words

Too long, it's been
And the noise breaks
Too long in sorrow
Cannot cross

A song is coming
Can find no rest
We cannot cross
Give us the words

Knew a man once
Had no tongue
Walked in fog
Till the fog was gone

It's been so long
Words cannot console us
Where there is sorrow
We cannot cross

Our souls are not for hire
Our loss is not for sale
We'll build a palace of tears and blood
On the fields of our enduring pain

It's been so long
Words cannot console us
Where there is sorrow
We cannot cross

A song is coming
Can find no rest
We cannot cross
Give us the words

Song is coming
Find no words
Cannot cross
Cannot cross

4. Indissolubility (Motetus absconditus)

There's no solution to the question if the question
becomes the solution.
Long walks deride the obvious intractability of any
mimesis.
When answers present themselves as this or that
It does not follow that the next step is to say
both/and or either/or.
Don't just rethink the problem rethink what pre-
cludes the question.
It is never just a matter of identification but of
recognition as refiguration.
It is never just a matter of recognition as refigura-
tion but redemption through resistance.

Tears sole dilution chews the winsome imp's affec-
tion's freedom's sheer incursion
Wrong quakes deprive the odious retractability of
aging oasis
Bent and swerved resent sham shelves at switch or
swat
Ill dots jog fallow tab dud vexed wept into weigh
sloth and pour eats her lore

Funk dusk hijinks tea probe fend be link shot de-
   ludes the jest done
Lit hiss sever trust a chatter of infantilization cuts or
   see fog's mission as recuperation
Lit hiss ever just a bladder of recuperation as infan-
   tilization guts exemption through insistence.

5. Amphibolies II (Noon) [instrumental]

noon
at thickest
are shadows where
stares the behind back you
take that
map
a on points are pricks
the briar
the
the paths into
over
quickly jump and
slowly walk

6. In the Dark (But Even Fire Is Light)

But it is cold anyway
even with the
fire and there
is never enough
light to see.

7. Sometimes

Sometimes
you burn a book because
it is cold
and you need the fire
to keep warm
and
sometimes
you read a
book for the same reason.
This is not a theory of reading
this is about staying alive
in a particular place and
a particular time.

This is not
because
you are weary of learning
but what it means to die
in a particular moment and
a particular space.

.

you are weary of learning
a particular time
a particular space
it is cold
this is about staying alive
you read a
in a particular place and
this is not a theory of reading
but what it means to die
and you need the fire
book for the same reason
in a particular moment and
This is not
to keep warm

because
sometimes
you burn a book because
and
sometimes

8. Anagrammatica

I'm a lent barn Jew
A mint bran jewel
A barn Jew melt in
A rent Jew in balm
A Jew lamb intern
Brain mantle Jew
Brain mental Jew
A bawl intern jem
Arab Jew melt inn
Blat ma inner Jew
Bam rat linen Jew
An altern IBM Jew
Ran tan lib Jew me
Balm at inner Jew
Rat bam Lenin Jew

Balm tear Jew inn
Atman Berlin Jew

9. dew and die

can dew and die can and die can tie his sin tap and
the war dew hoe and die has him and her and tar the
pry and war mud and bog and tug eye and has him and
her bug dew can dew sin tap can and not lie and the
eye wag and the can and the can not and can ire not
and war beg ire and war not beg ire and has out ire
him and her and die war tug for kin war for kin its
was for kin its mob tic and ken hot and tug dew ken
sob and sob hog beg hop for ire him and tug dew ken
can dew its tug art its was the its was the its for
sun not lie and gag tug the eye wag sub and hug but
pun end dew oar and tag irk hog and our wag nor gut
and nab and sub top tic rum and not lie pop ken arm
and gab his ken and the our and the hog and sad and
sit and sob tic ire tic his tic and the rot war lie
and die rut and dew tag wag tic eye and mud and woe
and not and dew ire and die his and sow hug irk hug
and hit and lug tie out the its gut its for sun and

lie and kin bob and dew rib and sob and die kin and
bug his nab and sub top tic rum and sow was dew and
dew lay out ire and sob and tar and rib and bob and
sow and ire arm and the hog sad and the our die rut
zen see and the amp irk and tot and wet for rim its
wag sit wag nor she out him and her him and him her
him her him her big rot and sob and woe die see sin
tap rib and bob and ken orb nab and mud lag out sun

10. *Schein*

There's no crime like the
shine in the space between
shine and shame.

•

No shine like the mine between meaning and
    history. No space
like the rime between shine and face. No rime
    like the
lace between time and memory.

11. Dusts to Dusks

The heavens turn dark before the trees are shot
   full of light.

12. Amphibolies III (Pricks)

Noon
thickest at
where shadows are
you back behind the stares
that take
map
pricks are points on a
briar. The
the
the paths into
over
and jump quickly
walk slowly

13. Salute

The blank sail of our soul [toll]
The blank toil of our sail [veil]
The blank soul of our toil [soil]

Notes

The title comes from "The Doctrine of the Similar" *[Die Lehre von Änlichkeit]*, the 1933 Benjamin essay that is a key source for the opera. The text is based on prime numbers, as counted in lines for each stanza and words per line.

1. "Amphibolies I (Walk Slowly)" (13): 13 lines of 1, 2, 3, and 5 words, followed by two sets of variants.

2. "Dust to Dusk": 11 words.

3. "Cannot Cross" (11): 11 stanzas.

4. "Indissolubility (Motetus Absconditus)" (7): 2 7-line stanzas. The second stanza is a homophonic transposition (translation) of the first stanza.

5. "Amphibolies II (Noon)" (13): 13 lines; variants of canon 1, "Amiphibolies 1." This section is performed as an instrumental.

6. "In the Dark (But Even Fire Is Light)" (5): 5 lines of 3s and 5s.

7. "Sometimes" (19): 19 lines of 1, 3, 5 and 7 words, followed by variant.

8. "Anagrammatica" (17): 17 lines (anagrams of walterbenjamin).

9. "dew and die" (13): 26 lines: 13 + 13. Structural/homophonic translation of "Der und Die" by Ernst Jandl.

10. "Schein" (3): 3 lines of primes, followed by variant.

11. "Dusts to Dusks": 11 words. Variant of canon 2, "Dust to Dusk." In performance, the text of canon 2 is sung, rather than this variant.

12. "Amphibolies III (Pricks)" (13): 13 lines, variants of canons 1 and 5.

13. "Salute" (3): 3 lines, variations of the last line of Mallarmé's poem "Salute": "Le blanc souci de notre toile."

IV. OPUS CONTRA NATURAM (DESCENT OF BENJAMIN INTO THE UNDERWORLD)

I.

Are the shadows of objects on cave walls
themselves objects?
Undecidable.

Do images read minds?
Semantic insufficiency.

Then as when, now as some what or other.
Corrupted data.

What's the cube root of a counterfactual?
An almond.

Palimpsestic forms, Cracked spines,
Archives of anteriority, Vampiric codes,
Bell, book and candle.
Henceforth unavailable.

2. Katabasis

... from time to time in time to time ...
... into and out of ...
... like as as as as as as like ...
... sealed off or shook up ...
... smack it ...
... or it'll zap you ...
... place your bets between the gaps ...
... is it real, or is it cropped ... ?
... lock it in a box and frame it with a clock ..
... stop it or it'll crack you ...
... stuff it or it'll sting you ...
... spin you ...
... does it frag or does it mock ... ?
... skin you ...
... pop it or get sucked up in ...
... stop it ...
... sock you ...
... out of ...
... or tock you ...
... like as ...
... as like ...
... as when ... between ... beside ... along ...

. . . knock knock who's there? don't ask don't tell
   who knows . . .

. . . the answer comes in the form of a question, an
   echo inside a

shadow wrapped in cellophane . . .

. . . or so the story's told.

3. Kataplexy

i.
not one avail ables lull to swell bell book cant
   to cant
tear end wip of or vamp ire
aim at vies crack spine on feign pal limp pest still
   sounds all
count err facts fail for falls in splint gel
the way the day tugs up by tads there
same as now minds bend sigh in some odd jests
   fold bets
or sun in stuff eye taints I meant
mind fled finds age as hem selves slit gnaw nor silt
old quests of shade O thou art told so
spore rails in cell plain as warps wrap shades
   in thrall

ii.

a cove a quest a form a comb a swerve a nod a shell
    a tear a taste
a long be side as like be twixt
who teal with smoke or was or as as time is tongues
    to tap a till or thrust nor tune or trill nor spare

iii.

to tear the time with shade or goad what fells fall

iv.

spook such pores in ups and whens which not
    to know spares got to
nor sway nor ban nor tip nor spark

v.

is calm where this no more to see than saw
you see is what you give where seam is torn and
    such says
as as as as as as as

vi.

now here not there now come now gone
like is is like as as is like nor

vii.

calm where there is no calm as balm where
there is no balm

suits the tale to swerve a thought nor lays a
frown to stay

viii.

now flash now flail now fail now sway now
swing now stray

Note

The text of part 1 is by Brian Ferneyhough.

V. POOLS OF DARKNESS
(11 INTERROGATIONS)

1. Three Giant Mouths
   (Canon/Heterophony)

GIANT MOUTHS:

Is the future a memory projected into time or is the past a shadow of a future that never happens?

WB:

The future is memory projected into time and the past is the future's way of forgetting.

GMS:

Why must the future already be inscribed in the past?

WB:

Only when time stops, only when the scales fall from our eyes, only when history is over, only when tales stop telling, only when the sun rises and sets in the same moment, only when nothing comes to nothing, only when we no longer look at the stars but are the stars …

GMS:
Why can't the past ever pass?

WB:
The past never passes but we pass over it again and again, not listening to what it tells but to the empty stories we tell about it.

2. Headless Ghoul
   (Isorhythmic Motet)

Are you waking from a dream or are you waking into a dream? Are you remembering your dreams or dreaming that you have memories?

[No reply by WB]

3. Two-headed figure of Karl Marx and Groucho
   Marx, with Kerberus
   (Hoquetus-Melodrama)

THE TWO MARXES (KARL):
Is it possible to forget without remembering
that one has forgotten?

WB:
As a child I mistook my a's for q's and d's for
f's. I looked for the signs between the letters.
Later I went to the university but the letters
were replaced by vowels which I could never
pronounce. I made my way and my way made
me.

THE TWO MARXES (GROUCHO):
Is it possible to remember without forgetting
what one has remembered?

WB:
The snow falls fresh but it is always soiled, yet
it's at dusk that my thoughts interrupt them-
selves.

THE TWO MARXES (GROUCHO):
Say the magic word and get one free ride around Alexanderplatz, say the magic letter and everybody returns to just as it is. A duck was crossing the strasse and the peacock said, Why a duck? Why a rabbit? Why a pipe? Why a carousel?

THE TWO MARXES (KARL):
How many lyrics does it take to make an epic? How many epics does it take to break an egg? How many eggs does it take to get from Ghent to Aix?

WB:
Take me behind the scenes and I will show you another scene and another after that, but the tiny man inside the works is no longer there, for he has gone off to work.

*

KERBERUS:

Why a duck?

Don't answer so fast or it will all be over before
you can say *Juden frei, Juden frei, can't see me!*

Nicht voreilig antworten, sonst wird alles vor-
bei sein, ehe du . . . sagen kannst *Juden frei, Ju-
den frei, can't see me!*

Mehr Licht, oder ziehst du die Dunkelheit vor,
my little kunst-maggot?

Come closer, but not that close.

Viens tout pres mais pas trop pres.

Acércate pero no tanto.

Naeherertreten, aber nicht so nahe.

4. Pope Pius XII
   (Dramatic Madrigal a due)

POPE PIUS XII:
Why didn't you take a gun and blast them out of this world?

WB:
I have always maintained a modicum of reflection is worth an infinite amount of later adjustment.

PP:
Why didn't you swing and shoot and go down in a flame of transcendent immolation?

WB:
The soul is no place for a football game.

PP:
Is this the way God has chosen to punish you for your sins?

WB:
Even sleeping dogs howl in pain.

5. Joan of Arc
   (Palimpsestic Chorale)

JOAN OF ARC:
If history never sleeps then are you the demon
of the wakefulness to which we are forever im-
prisoned? Is forever a bullet or a bracket or a
brace? By not telling do you consign us to un-
certainty or to abjection?

WB *(simultaneous or overlapping):*
If history never sleeps then are you the demon
of the wakefulness to which we are forever im-
prisoned? Is forever a bullet or a bracket or a
brace? By not telling do you consign us to un-
certainty or to abjection?

6. Baal Shem Tov Disguised as Vampire
   (Rebus)

BAAL SHEM TOV:
Is allegory better than symbolism?

WB:
No

BST:
Is symbolism better than reproduction?

WB:
No

BST:
Is reproduction better than tragedy?

WB:
No

BST:
Is tragedy better than alarm?

WB:
No

BST:
Is alarm better than aversion?

WB:
No

BST:
Is aversion better than engagement?

WB:
No

BST:
Is engagement better than detachment?

WB:
No

BST:
Is detachment better than assimilation?

WB:
No

BST:
Is assimilation better than estrangement?

WB:
No

BST:
Is estrangement better than allegory?

WB:
No

BST:
Is allegory better than symbolism?

WB:
No

BST:
Is symbolism better than reproduction?

WB:
No

BST:
Is reproduction better than tragedy?

WB:
No

BST:
Is tragedy better than alarm?

WB:
No

BST:
Is alarm better than aversion?

WB:
No

BST:
Is aversion better than engagement?

WB:
No

BST:
Is engagement better than detachment?

WB:
No

BST:
Is detachment better than assimilation?

WB:
No

BST:
Is assimilation better than estrangement?

WB:
No

BST:
Is estrangement better than allegory?

WB:
No

(round: back to beginning)

7. Adolf Hitler
   (Rondo)

ADOLF HITLER:

Can you go nowhere? Be no place? Come into nothing? Can you hold air? Can you be transfixed by transitions alone? Can you embrace the aimless? Embody ether? Lose yourself without finding another? Can you be numb to necessity and insensible to sobriety? Wander and not be alone? Be alone and not wonder?

WB *(simultaneous)*:

No telling what comes if you deny the unforeseen or abrade the collocation of no time in which to return without telling, submerging by the elocution of misplaced equations. Drown the boat and the sea sweeps over the waves. Ground the boat and the straws upend the beginning – the beginning you never had but to tumble, silly to say other than fumble.

8. Albert Einstein
   (Passacaglia cum Figuris in Eco)

   What time is it *now?* What time is it *now?*
   What time is it *now?* What time is it *now?*
   What time is it *now?* What time is it *now?*
   What time is it *now?* What time is it *now?*
   What time is it *now?* What time is it *now?*
   What time is it *now?* What time is it *now?*...

   [no reply by WB]

9. Border Guard
   (Pastoral Interlude)

   BORDER GUARD:
   Name?

   WB:
   Walter Benjamin

BG:
Date of birth?

WB:
15 July 1892

BG:
Address?

WB:
Undetermined

BG:
Education?

WB:
Doctor of Philosophy

BG:
Employment?

WB:
Undetermined

BG:
Race, Mother?

WB:
Reform

BG:
Race, Father?

WB:
Merchant

10. Four Furies
(Fugato)

FURIES:
What is to be done?

WB:
The light spills into pools of darkness. I can no
longer find it.

11. Golem
(Quodlibet / Abgesangszena)

GOLEM:
Infantibicia oag reboo nebullia sob expleanur
gendithany?

WB:
If not by running then by walking if not by
walking then by climbing if not by climbing
then by sliding if not by sliding then by stalling.

GOLEM:
Aulobby forsbick fenump inscriprit eggibus
murmertz ugum veh egbit vorum?

WB:
Leave them alone and they'll come home or
fiddle till the morning come no more.

GOLEM:
Phiantiup okum truggy do vestidat doorusium
uya?

WB:

Neither in the company of those who you do not know at all or in the company of those you know too well.

GOLEM:

Feefa, feega oow iggly?

WB:

If I submit then I die.

GOLEM:

Oraasamay dodofelliu ferumptious?

WB:

The street is neither inside nor outside, as rocks roll when you toss them down a hill and the name on the door says no one at home.

GOLEM:

Fogum, fogum are be gridit etsey?

WB:

First you know it, then not. That's when you begin to find out.

GOLEM:

Felum nevisier obit entripier? Acker muh obli-
um vodobillium seraybit illium? Illium squapos
meta? Fundodio inderrfolk oleptic fundy?

WB:

Keine Kaddish wird man sagen.

Note

The final line of this scene is from the German-Jewish post-
Romantic poet Heinrich (born Harry) Heine (1797-1856),
whose work was often censored and, indeed, was banned
by the Nazis. Two poems by Heine figure significantly in
Scene VI. Benjamin, while hardly identifying with Heine's
work, believed him to be a distant relative. And both Ben-
jamin and Heine found themselves exiled in Paris. The line
could be translated, "No one to say Kaddish for me": the
lament of a secular, or assimilated, Jew. Louis Zukofsky
ends the second movement of "A Poem Beginning 'The'"
with this citation of Heine.

VI. SEVEN TABLEAUX VIVANTS REPRESENTING THE ANGEL OF HISTORY AS MELANCHOLIA (SECOND BARRIER)

1. Laurel's Eyes

> Each night is soul-bedeviled
> As each frayed ship rigs sail
> In journey's end sight falters
> Where journey never ends
>
> A draught so thin it's bitter
> A ruin like the Rhine
> That rips its fleece in kilter
> Abandoned to its shine
>
> The shone star yearns for light
> Door opens, wonder barred
> Ire's golden gate gets blistered
> Seek comet, err in folded heart

Seek comet, err in folded heart
And drink a daft farewell
That has its blunder tendered
In quivering, feathered tar

Sifted in climate's sieve
Engrafts its festooned way
As spark ignites the weave
And shouts ordain the play

This globe spins on, verse lingers
A sail without a sigh
A song without a singer
Laurel's veil, Laurel's eyes

2. Tensions

each ear's sly fiction a toy taboo which founds
us

fear begets gain in trust 'til thwarts anew bogus
delay

pale cheer wanes in crust of fabled dew's mo-
ment's bending

wants well as wills fell mordant sense of sent-
up hopes

slide at diction fences sapped affliction in tents
not flinches

sipped affection moves impatience over hood-
ed hounded hapless hallowed hills

missed obsession slips bided glance at torsion's
tabbed tattooed surround

tear's friction cobbles fact for tarnished shame's
shunned shuttered wince

fist courts hocus-pocus display as depth rico-
chets side-saddle

bent torts ape discordant art's hue lending ut-
ter addled sap

3. Hashish in Marseilles

These stones are the bread
of imagination. Reading the notices
on the urinals, *things withstand my
gaze*. Such joy in the mere act
of unrolling a ball of thread. One becomes
tender, fearing that a shadow falling on
paper might hurt it. It's too noisy here.
I must note how I found my place.
Seeing only nuances. As when
the intensity of acoustic impressions
blots out all others. The solitude of such
trances works as a filter. Yet I am disturbed
by a child crying.

*

Am I yet disturbed
filter, work of trance, such solitude,
others blots, impressions
of acoustic intensity whose
nuances only see traces, my notes
founder here, noisy, too

hurt might paper a fall that shows
a fear, tender becomes one
thread of balls unrolling, act
in joy such gaze, my things
which stand, urinals of notice,
reading imagination of bread, stones,
these …

*

Bread is stone
withstanding thread
sheer toys such maze
becomes threat unruling
oily shadow
cozy vapor
where fluency mars
impressions
as tested falter

4. After Heine

Capital is the fool's gold
Labor is the folded haze
It's dark now, I'm sleeping
Work's made me tired

Over my heart grows a web
Which traps the weary Nightingale
She sings of only history
I hear it even in sleep

5. One and a Half Truths

In the weeks ahead, we lag behind. The
Bear sees the cantaloupe only at the
Filling station. Hope grows feathers when it
Loses its antennae. The earth is a
Bootblack that prefers magenta. Just a-
Round the corner is another corner.
Just around the corner is the coron-
Er. Fresh fruit is better than oily pa-
Jamas. Light is the furthest thing from mind
When the operating system is down-
Loaded. A cup is not always a cup.
Keep your mittens posted. Some allergies
Are unforgivable. A house on a
Hill makes a good target. Make beans while the

Hay dries. Money is the root of all cur-
Rency. If it works in the office try
Gatorade. The evolution of the
Species is a form of infanticide.
A pound of bleach is worth almost nothing.
Bleach yourself before you bleach others.
  Bleach
Yourself and the whole world looks pale. The
  trick
Is in the trust not the lock. Jimmie with
A square and you'll get pizza. The plaza
Is surrounded by walruses. Ice blue
But not forgotten. Never mistake a
Feather for a pirate. Second glances
Are always first in line. Shimmers rule. Truth
Is a gun loaded with a parachute.

6. Can'ts

if you can't see it it can still hurt you

you can't see if it can it hurt you still

can't if can you you still see it it hurt

see it still you hurt you can't it can if

it still you if see hurt it can can't you

it you it can if you see hurt can't still

can it still can't if you it hurt you see

(if you it can if you see hurt can't still)

still hurt can't you see it if it you can

hurt it still you can't see can you if it

you hurt still can can't you see it if it

7.

Madame Moiselle and Mr. Moiselle
Went for a walk with their gazelle.

The tiger slept on the sewing machine
And all the children swept themselves clean.

Rings of desire, floods of wisps
Who's to say what, what's to say which
Whether what is is so because
Or whether what is is not

Who's to say, what's to say
Whether what is is not
Or whether what is is so because
Is so because it's not

Notes

In the performance score for "Seven Tableaux Vivants,"
cuts have been made in sections 3 and 5.

1. The underlying layer of the lyric is a homophonic trans-
lation of Heine's "Die Lorelei" (1823):

Ich weiß nicht, was soll es bedeuten,
Daß ich so traurig bin;
Ein Märchen aus alten Zeiten,

Das kommt mir nicht aus dem Sinn.
Die Luft ist kühl und es dunkelt,
Und ruhig fließt der Rhein;
Der Gipfel des Berges funkelt
Im Abendsonnenschein.
Die schönste Jungfrau sitzet
Dort oben wunderbar;
Ihr goldnes Geschmeide blitzet,
Sie kämmt ihr goldenes Haar.
Sie kämmt es mit goldenem Kamme
Und singt ein Lied dabei;
Das hat eine wundersame,
Gewaltige Melodei.
Den Schiffer im kleinen Schiffe
Ergreift es mit wildem Weh;
Er schaut nicht die Felsenriffe,
Er schaut nur hinauf in die Höh.
Ich glaube, die Wellen verschlingen
Am Ende Schiffer und Kahn;
Und das hat mit ihrem Singen
Die Lorelei getan.

There have been over 25 musical settings of Heine's poem. The best known are the folkloric version by Friedrich Silcher and the art song version by Franz Liszt. Mark Twain wrote about the Lorelei legend in *A Tramp Abroad* and did his own translation of Heine's poem – "She combs with a comb that is golden, / And sings a weird refrain / That steeps in a deadly enchantment / The list'ner's ravished brain." One of Sylvia Plath's most haunting poems, "Lorelei," involves a radical transformation of the psychic and gender dynamics of Heine's poem – "Sisters, your song / Bears a burden too weighty / For the whorled ear's listening." Both the Gershwins and The Pogues wrote Lorelei "covers." The legend usually begins with a girl, cruelly abandoned by her lover, throwing herself into the Rhine. By some magic, beyond rational powers of understanding, the drowned maiden is reborn as a Siren (or mermaid-like creature), who, in the forever after of the song, lures fishermen to their ruin on the Lorelei cliff, to the background music of the crash of the waves against the rocks. Note: In the performance score, the last line is not recited.

2. Ten by ten, with each of the lines working with sounds from the previous lines. The first line is derived in part from the word string in section 6, all of whose letters can be reassembled to make "each ear's sly fiction toy tutu I unlit."

3. "Hashish in Marseilles" is based on Benjamin's 1932 essay, translated by Edmund Jephcott and collected in *Walter Benjamin: Selected Writings*, Volume 2: 1927-1934 (Cambridge, Mass.: Harvard University Press, 1999), pp. 673-679. The second section works through the first section backwards.

4. A reworking of Heine's "Der Tod, das ist die kühle Nacht" –

Death is the Cool Night

Death is the cool Night
Life the muggy Day
It's dark already, I'm sleepy
Day's made me tired

Over my bed grows a Tree
Where sings the young Nightingale;
She sings of only Love
I hear it even in Dream

(my translation)

5. I take the title of this double sonnet from Karl Kraus's collection of aphorisms. The 27 sentences (or some subset) could be reordered for extension or echo.

6. The second 10 x 10; the first line determines the first word of each subsequent line; each line uses the same word set. The sixth line is repeated, with odd variant.

VII. STELAE FOR FAILED TIME (SOLO FOR MELANCHOLIA AS THE ANGEL OF HISTORY)

Albrecht Dürer, *Melencolia*

First Layer

Just as I
no sooner than
I had seen you
for the first time
journeyed back
with you
from where I came
and the faces I saw
had disappeared
unable to trace
what I had known
too long
just as you
journeyed back
with me
no sooner than
we met
where you fell
for the first time
hardly to face
the facts I saw
what I had known

always disappearing
and the places
you saw
unable to trace
what's known
then gone
just as I
journeyed back
with you
no sooner than
I held you
from where I came
for the last time
never to face
the facts I saw
what I had
forgotten
now whispers
just as you
no sooner than
you touched me
the first time
journeyed back
with me

to where
I am.

Tvòdlÿ-uxìs kanq' otmì
V'xùq'iÿ-uxìs kanq'otmì
Çàv vu-desìvelotmiutvut
Vuq'çùq'iÿ-vun çisèli

Blame is a child's game
played by men
in the furor
of their discontent.

Tef-mux
Naf-johj
Nuvjis-vun vu-vmimòtmi
Vu jùnië-vu zi-dumfàdvotlit

Beyond the despair
is the listlessness
of not. The shipwreck
of the arational
on the shores of
the promised. This is

where I
founder, disappearing
into tears *[tarz]*, hidden
in the masks
of the victor's
tears *[teerz]*.

Vu, ini-tomàmotu
Dev vuq'hàï-vun zo-jetotù
Vuq'ni vjisìgusi vi-hoxiòtmi

Blame a child's game
Played by men
In the bureaus
Of their contempt

Vùq'uàv-oq' ke-oq'-ùâv
'Qìhojçus-inìn tjìf za-otuòm
òlië-çumùf hoq' za-foslòtu

Deep in the heavens, high on the breeze
I told the examiner, found the key
Went to the opening, key didn't fit
Forged another, it got ripped

First there's a tumble, then there's a sash
So irksome you scratch it, scratch till it's ash
Losing the battles, winning the war
Sinking in quicksand when you can think at all

Sometimes look back, sometimes set fires
Who's to judge? No one's above desire.
The monkeys you are, the angels you'll be
When truth comes to lashes, when language is weed

Xomhÿ-vun
Tq'esÿ-him vu-çièvotmi
Xis vu-otlì
Vu-g'mèmok

I back away
helpless, my eyes fixed.
This is my task:
to imagine no wholes
from all that has been smashed.

For now time is lost, now time is
cracked, now time is empty, now
time is framed, now time is lived,

now time is hollow, now time
is smoked, now time is stolen.

And the new angels pass away
like sparks on coals

Just as we
no sooner than
we had seen each other
for the first time
journeyed back together
from where we came.

For now time is lost
now time is gained
now time is empty
now time is full
now time is lived
now time is hollow
now time is made
now time is stone.

Second Layer

The best picture
of a picture
is not a picture
but the negative.
The negative pictures
the picture
just as I
picture you
without ever seeing
the picture
you see
as your reflection.
What can't be seen
is still
apprehended
even as I lose more
than I retain
as I go
backwards
in time toward
time's end.
Keeping still

I misplace
the picture
of the picture
tossed in tales
of the rune
of the telling
unraveling
the threads
that hold
the leaves
scattering
the frieze.
The best picture
of a picture
is not the picture
but its reverse
rehearsing tales
until they
unfold
in the tolling
even as I regret
more than I
resemble
in the tumble

of my apprehensive
incomprehending.
The negative pictures
the picture better
than the picture
just as I
picture you
without
ever having seen you
or touched you
as now you fall
from my arms
into my capacious
insomniac forgetting.

Shadowtime was commissioned by the City of Munich in 1999 for the Munich Biennale in coproduction with the Festival d'Automne, Paris; the Ruhrtriennale, Gelsenkirchen; and the Lincoln Center Festival, New York. In addition, the following organizations provided commissions for specific compositions: Carnegie Hall Corporation (scene 3), the Flanders Festivals and Ian Pace (scene 4), the Musée d'Orsay and the Ensemble InterContemporain (scene 6), and Jean-Philippe and Françoise Billarant for the IRCAM (scene 7). The production in Munich was realized in collaboration with the Bayerische Theaterakademie August Everding.

World premiere on Tuesday, May 25, 2004, at Prinzregententheater, Munich.

Music: Brian Ferneyhough
Libretto: Charles Bernstein

Musical director: Jurjen Hempel
Director: Frédéric Fisbach
Set designer: Emanuel Clolus
Costumes: Olga Karpinsky

Light Design: Marie-Christine Soma
Dramaturge: Benoit Résillot

Neue Vocalsolisten Stuttgart
Nieuw Ensemble Amsterdam
Solo performers:
Nicolas Hodges (piano/speaker)
Mats Scheidegger (guitar)
Ekkehardt Abele, bass-baritone
    (Walter Benjamin)
Angelika Luz, soprano
    (Innkeeper/interrogator)
Monika Meier-Schmid, soprano
    (Dora Benjamin/interrogator)
Janet Collins, alto
    (Henny Gurland/interrogator)
Sabine Schilling, mezzo-soprano
    (child, interrogator)
Christiane Schmelling, mezzo-soprano (child)
Martin Nagy, tenor (Hölderlin, interrogator)
Bernard Gärtner, tenor (interrogator)
Frank Bossert, tenor (interrogator)
Stefan Weible, tenor
Guillermo Anzorena, baritone
    (young Walter Benjamin, interrogator)

Andreas Fischer, bass
    (Gershom Scholem, interrogator)
Matthias Horn, bass (interrogator)
Tobias Schlierf, bass

GREEN INTEGER
Pataphysics and Pedantry

Douglas Messerli, *Publisher*

Essays, Manifestos, Statements, Speeches, Maxims,
Epistles, Diaristic Notes, Narratives, Natural Histories,
Poems, Plays, Performances, Ramblings, Revelations
and all such ephemera as may appear necessary
to bring society into a slight tremolo of confusion
and fright at least.

*

Green Integer Books